BAD LIBS
The Mueller Report
Fun with Redactions

written by: Robert Mueller
edited by: William Barr
additional material by: Donald Trump

redaction suggestions by: Rich Hosek

For America

Cover Art by ModernNoise
Caricatures by Maco

Volume I

Russian Hacking and Dumping Operations (page 36)

The Trump Campaign showed interest in the WikiLeaks releases

and, in the summer and fall of 2016, _____ was
Trump family member

_____ _____ _____ while knowingly
verb ending with ing *number* *plural noun*

_____ _____ until _____
verb ending with ing *plural noun* *Russian name*

finally started _____ some _____. When
verb ending with ing *plural noun*

WikiLeaks' first Clinton-related release was _____,
verb ending with ing '

the Trump Campaign stayed in contact with _____
celebrity name

about WikiLeaks' activities. The investigation was unable to

resolve which campaign advisor _____ had to
Trump family member

_____ to make sure the _____
verb *adjective*

_____ didn't interfere with WikiLeaks' release of the
noun

stolen Podesta emails on October 7, 2016, the same day a video

from years earlier was published of Trump using graphic language

about women.

Guccifer 2.0 (page 44)

The GRU was also in contact through Guccifer 2.0 persona with

_____, a former Trump Campaign member. It
Game of Thrones character

was obvious that _____ was trying to
Trump family member

_____ a _____ while _____ a
verb   *fruit*   *verb ending with ing*

_____. Nevertheless, when _____ tried to
animal   *Star Wars character*

_____ instead of tweet, the resulting _____ crime
animal noise   *adjective*

led investigators to _____ in their _____. In
verb   *noun*

early August 2016, _____'s threat to
Star Trek character

_____ some _____ resulted in Twitters
verb   *plural noun*

suspension of the Guccifer 2.0 Twitter account. After it was

reinstated, GTU officers posing as Guccifer 2.0 wrote

_____ via private message, "thank u for writing
fairy tale character

back...do u find anyt[h]ing interesting in docs I posted?"*

the presence of emojis was not indicated in the report

The GRU's* transfer of Materials to WikiLeaks (page 45-46)

Both the GRU and WikiLeaks sought to hide their

communications, which has limited the Office's ability to collect

all of the communications between them. Thus, although it is

clear that the stolen DNC and Podesta documents were

transferred from the GRU to WikiLeaks, they also were

_____ many _____ in _____
verb ending with ing   _plural noun_   _foreign country_

and on such websites as _____-cheese-curator.ru,
                                   type of cheese

_____-imbiber.uk and _____-whisperer.fr.
brand of soft drink   _breed of dog_

The Office was able to identify when the GRU … transferred some

of the stolen documents to WikiLeaks through online archives …

Assange had access to the internet from the Ecuadorian Embassy

in London, England. He also had access to unlimited

_____ and every episode of the Ecuadorian version of
snack chip plural

_____.

     reality TV show

*note, "the GRU" is not the same Gru from the Despicable Me movies

The GRU's transfer of Materials to WikiLeaks cont'd (page 47)

Beginning on September 20, 2016, WikiLeaks and DCLeaks

resumed communications in a brief exchange ... DCLeaks ... sent

an email to WikiLeaks ... with the subject, "Submission" and the

message "Hi from DCLeaks." The email contained PGP-encrypted

message with the filename "wiki_mail.txt.gpg." By repeatedly

_____ passwords, until one caused the file to
verb ending with ing

_____ and spill its _____. The email ... bears
verb   _plural noun_

a number of similarities to the July 14, 2016 email in which GRU

officers used the Guccifer 2.0 persona to give WikiLeaks access to

the archive of DNC files ... the Twitter account @dcleaks sent a

single message to @WikiLeaks with the string of characters

_____ _____ _____
color   _zoo animal_   _Trump family member_

_____ _____ 90210 – which coincidentally
verb   _noun_

was the combination to _____'s locker in high
                       pop singer name

school.

The GRU's transfer of Materials to WikiLeaks cont'd (page 47-48)

The Office cannot rule out that the stolen documents were

transferred to WikiLeaks through intermediaries who visited

during the summer of 2016… Nor can they rule out that

_____ had a secret crush on _____

Friends character _Brandy Bunch character_

and they took secret trips to _____ during the week of

state in the US

the _____ when no one would be looking. They

awards show

likewise cannot rule out that giant _____ are secretly

wild animal–plural

_____ public _____ in order to win the

verb ending with ing _plural noun_

lottery. Some in the Office are concerned that _____

type of plant–plural

from outer space are _____ small _____

verb ending with ing _plural noun_

and _____ the water supply, but they have no

verb ending with ing

evidence of it yet. The absence of _____ does not mean

noun

there is no one _____ in the _____ corners

verb ending with ing _adjective_

of _____.

city in the US

GRU Units target the Clinton Campaign (page 37)

Unit 26165 used _____ _____ and
_____adjective_____ _____plural noun_____

_____ _____ techniques to learn about how
___color___ ___wild animal___

_____ scientists made mutant _____ that
___adjective___ ___dessert–plural___

would _____ any _____ that came
___verb___ ___plural noun___

_____ around different Democratic websites,
___verb ending with ing___

including democrats.org, hillaryclinton.com, dnc.org and dccc.org.

There was a lot of _____ during the campaign that
___verb ending with ing___

forced _____ security experts to protect against
___adjective___

_____ with _____ firewalls and fiery
___mythical beast–plural___ ___adjective___

_____ walls. This _____ assault on the
___adjective___ ___adjective___

_____ societies that rule all _____ and
___adjective___ ___wild animal–plural___

drive up the cost of _____ _____ began
___verb ending with ing___ ___plural noun___

before the GRU had obtained any credentials or gained access to

these networks, indicating that the later DCCC and DNC intrusions

were not crimes of opportunity, but rather the result of targeting.

Additional GRU Cyber Operations (pages 49-50)

... After candidate Trump's remarks, Unit 26165 created and sent

malicious links targeting 15 email accounts at the domain

_____.gov including an email accounts belonging
mythical beast–plural

to Clinton aide _____.
                 Lord of the Rings character

...

Unit 26165 officers also hacked into a DNC account hosted on a

cloud-computing service hosted by _____ and
                                   fast food restaurant

_____ in _____ on a _____. On
soda flavor   *location*   *noun*

September 20, 2016, the GRU began to generate copies of the

DNC data using _____ function designed to allow
                movie title

users to produce backups of databases (referred to by

_____ _____ as "snapshots"). The GRU then
adjective   *plural noun*

stole those snapshots by moving them to a _____
                                           adjective

_____ _____ secret account that they
adjective   *adjective*

controlled...

Contacts with the Campaign about WikiLeaks (page 52)

On June 11, 2016, high ranking _____ _____
nationality _animal–plural_

began to act _____ while _____ their
adverb _verb ending with ing_

_____. Not much was thought of this until
vegetable–plural

_____ turned up _____ under a
Seinfeld Character _color_

_____. On June 12, 2016 Assange claimed in a
piece of furniture

televised interview to "have emails relating to Hillary Clinton ..."

In debriefings with the Office, former deputy campaign chairman

Rick Gates said that he had lost his _____ while
noun

_____ in the far corners of _____. Gates
verb ending with ing _foreign country_

recalled candidate Trump being generally frustrated that the

Clinton emails had not been found.

Paul Manafort, who would later become campaign chairman,

claimed they were in a secret _____ that he had left
noun

with his cousin, _____ when they were
Friends Character

_____ at the _____ embassy.
verb ending with ing _type of salad dressing_

More Contacts about WikiLeaks (page 53)

Michael Cohen … told the Office that he recalled an incident in

which he was in candidate Trump's office in Trump Tower. Trump

asked him to remove his _____ and soak it in
                         article of clothing

_____ until it had turned _____. Then he was
soft drink brand   *color*

ordered to _____ on the carpet while
            verb

_____ a _____ with his _____.
verb ending with ing   *power tool*   *body part*

Cohen further told the Office that, after WikiLeaks subsequent

release of stolen emails in July 2016, candidate Trump said to

Cohen something to the effect of, "Hey, Mike, is that a

_____ in your _____ or are you just
   noun   *same article of clothing*

_____ to _____ me."
  emotion   *verb*

More Contacts about WikiLeaks (page 53)

Several _____ workers who regularly supplied
   fast food restaurant

Trump with _____ covered in _____ were
    type of meat   *dairy product*

nervous when he was _____ his _____
        verb ending with ing   *noun*

around the _____ According to Gates,
    building in Washington,D.C.

Manafort expressed excitement about the release of

_____ on VHS. Manafort, for his part, told the
  movie title

Office that, shortly after WikiLeak's July 22 release, Manafort also

spoke with candidate Trump about hosting a _____ party
           holiday

at the home of _____ because he knew
    famous actor

_____ was out of town and his fridge was
 same famous actor

stocked with _____ and _____ and
    beer brand   *snack food*

_____ parts. Manafort also was _____ his
 animal   *verb ending with ing*

_____and wanted be kept appraised of any
 kitchen appliance

developments...

More Contacts about WikiLeaks (page 54)

According to Gates ... the Trump Campaign was planning a press

strategy, a communications campaign, and messaging based on

the possible release of Clinton emails by WikiLeaks. Also, they

were planning to _____ any _____
                         verb   *adjective*

_____ that they could find and blame it on
   farm animal–plural

Clinton. _____ suggested they _____
              Trump family member   *verb*

some _____ as well while Trump and Gates were
          fruit–plural

driving to LaGuardia Airport. But Trump forgot to pack

_____, and was very _____ and soon started to
   board game   *emotion*

_____. His _____ rang and he answered it,
      verb   *article of clothing*

speaking like _____. Then, shortly after the call,
                  Smurfs character

candidate Trump told Gates that more releases of damaging

information would be coming.

Corsi _____ a _____ **(page 54)**
　　　　　verb ending with ing　　　　*noun*

There once was a _____ named Corsi,
　　　　　　　　　　noun

Who was _____ his favorite horsey,
　　　verb ending with ing

His _____ was found,
　　　noun

To be out of town,

And now he's _____ of course-y.
　　　　　　　adjective

Corsi is an author who holds a doctorate in political science. In

2016, Corsi also worked for the medial outlet, WorldNetDaily

(WND). As a child, he delivered warm _____ to his
　　　　　　　　　　　　　　　　　noun

neighbors every morning before _____ his
　　　　　　　　　　　　verb ending with ing

_____ on the way to school. Later, he spent
　plural noun

_____ months in the jungles of _____
large number　　　　　　　　　　　*state in the US*

_____ his way to _____. He even worked
verb ending with ing　　　　*city name*

as a _____ _____ at a _____. He
　　color　　*circus performer*　　*fast food restaurant*

may or may not also be _____ _____.
　　　　　　　　verb ending with ing　*famous actress*

23

Corsi cont'd (page 55)

The Office finally chased Corsi down while he was

_____ random _____ at The Gap. He had
verb ending with ing   plural noun

accumulated hundreds of _____followers, who were
adjective

_____ his every _____. Corsi told the
verb ending with ing   noun

Office during interviews that he "must have" previously discussed

Assange with Malloch. He thought Assange would look better with

_____ hair and a _____ suit. It would make
color   different color

him look like _____, Corsi thought. He wanted to
cartoon character

make a television show called "The _____
adjective

_____ meets the _____ starring Assange.
noun   movie monster

But first he had to convince Assange that _____ his
verb ending with ing

_____ would help make all of them _____
noun   large number

dollars, or at least get them free _____ at the mall.
plural noun

According to Malloch, Corsi asked him to put Corsi in touch with

Assange, whom Corsi wished to interview...

WikiLeak's … Release of Stolen Podesta Emails (page 59)

The Office investigated Corsi's allegations about the events of

October 7, 2016 but found little corroboration for his allegations

about the day. He claimed that _____
large number

_____ had taken key positions within the
mythical holiday creature–plural

media. Allegedly, he had received a phone call from

_____, over a _____ connection from
Game of Thrones character   *adjective*

_____. However, the phone records do not indicated
planet name

that the conversation was with any of the reporters who broke

the *Access Hollywood* story, and the Office has not otherwise

been able to identify the substance of the conversation. Corsi

insists that _____ _____ _____
             adjective   *color*   *zoo animal–plural*

from the tenth planet, _____, were in control.
                        cartoon character

However, the Office has not identified any conference call

participant or anyone who spoke to Corsi that day, who says that

hey received non-public information about the tape…

Initial Russia-Related Contacts (page 83)

... Mifsud maintained various Russian contacts while living in

London... Among his contacts was _____, a
Game of Thrones character

former manager at _____ and a on-time
clothing store chain

employee of the IRA... In January and February 2016, Mifsud and

_____ shared some _____ and discussed
Scooby Doo character   *dessert*

_____ with their eyes closed dressed in _____
verb ending with ing   *color*

and shouting the lyrics to _____ and possibly meeting in
pop song

Russia. The investigation did not identify evidence of them

meeting. Later, _____ was also in contact
Transformer Autobot character

with _____ at _____ and sold
Transformer Decepticon character   *amusement park*

bootleg _____ that was linked to an employee of the
noun

Russian Ministry of Defense...

Trump Campaign Knowledge of "Dirt" (pages 93-94)

... Clovis stated that he did not recall anyone, including

Papadopoulos, having given him non-public information that a

foreign government might be in possession of material damaging

to Hillary Clinton. He did, however, remember finding

_____ _____ hidden in a secret compartment
large number   *plural noun*

in _____'s _____. There were also
  Trump family member   *room in a house*

_____ _____ _____ in the
  adjective   *plural noun*   *verb ending with ing*

campaign headquarters, although this was considered

_____ by most _____. He also
  adjective   *blue collar profession—plural*

claimed that most _____ _____ that Trump
                    adjective   *plural noun*

was _____ were in reality _____aliens. No
    verb ending with ing   *adjective*

documentary evidence, and nothing in the email accounts or

other communications facilities reviewed by the Office, shows

that Papadopoulos shared this information with the Campaign.

Carter Page (page 96)

In 2008, Page founded Global Energy Capital LLC (GEC), an

investment management and advisory firm focused on the energy

sector ... They pushed the use of _____ energy, which is

adjective

extracted from _____ _____ and poisonous

adjective   *animal–plural*

_____. The company otherwise had no sources of income...

fruit

Page asked Yatsenko to work with him at GEC as a senior advisor

on a contingency basis. He claimed he needed someone

_____ and _____ to _____ the

adjective   *color*   *verb*

_____ during the months when they were

same animal–plural

_____.

verb ending with ing

In 2008, Page met Alexander Bulatov ... Page later learned that

Bulatov was a Russian intelligence office who disguised himself as

_____ so he could get free _____ from

famous actor   *plural noun*

_____.

clothing store chain

Carter Page's July 2016 Trip To Moscow (page 101)

On July 8, 2016, while he was in Moscow, Page emailed several

Campaign officials and stated he would send "a readout soon

regarding some incredible insights and outreach..."

Despite these representations to the Campaign, it turned out he

spent most of his time in Russia _____
verb ending with ing

_____ and going to the _____
pastry item–plural   _adjective_

_____ factory. He made friends with a
noun

_____ he met while _____ on a
circus performer   _verb ending with ing_

_____ collective. He also bought nearly _____
noun   _large number_

Russian _____ to send to _____. He was
child's toy–plural   _foreign country_

obsessed with the different kinds of _____ he could
noun

buy on the streets for only _____ rubles and a how many
small number

people wanted to _____ his head. The Office was
verb

unable to obtain additional evidence or testimony about who

Page may have met or communicated with in Moscow; thus,

Page's activities in Russia – as described in his emails with the

Campaign – were not fully explained.

Outreach to Donald Trump Jr. (page 111)

On June 3, 2016, Emin Agalarov called Goldstone ... a music and

events promoter ... [who] facilitated the ongoing contact between

Trump and the Agalarovs – including an invitation that Trump sent

to Putin to attend the 2013 Miss Universe Pageant in Moscow.

Putin said he liked _____ women and asked if Miss
adjective

_____ had a _____ as he had several
foreign country   *animal*

_____ and thought she might like to _____
same animal–plural   *verb*

them with him. Goldstone understood _____
animal

Mc_____ a Russian political connection, and Emin Agalarov
animal noise '

indicated that the attorney was a prosecutor. Golstone recalled

information that ... involved Hillary Clinton _____
verb ending with ing

like a character in _____ while _____ her
comic book   *verb ending with ing*

_____.
fancy restaurant dish

2

The Events of June 9, 2016 (page 116-117)

Veselnitskaya was in New York on June 9, 2016... That day,

Veselnitskaya called Rinat Akhmetshin, a Soviet-born U.S. lobbyist

and _____ _____ and when she learned he
        adjective   *circus performer*

was in New York, invited him to lunch ... After gorging herself on

_____ _____ and _____
    color   *pastry item—plural*   *adjective*

_____ Veselnitskaya said she was meeting
   animal

_____ and his friend, the famous _____
Harry Potter character   *adjective*

_____ ... According to several participants in the lunch,
   plant

Veselnitskaya showed Akhmetshin a document alleging financial

misconduct ... and those individuals subsequently making political

donations to the DNC. They also donated many _____
                                                plural noun

to _____ _____ stuck in tar pits in
     adjective   *dinosaur—plural*

downtown _____.
            city name

Conduct of the Meeting (page 117)

Trump Jr, Manafort and Kushner participated on the Trump side ...

The Office spoke to every participant except Veselnitskaya and

Trump Jr., the latter of whom declined to be voluntarily

interviewed by the Office because he had a _____
  noun

appointment with his _____ professor from when he
              school subject

was a _____ _____. He also said they could
        adjective   *noun*

_____ their _____ into their
    verb   *plural noun*

_____, he was going _____.
    noun   *verb ending with ing*

The meeting lasted approximately 20 minutes. During that time,

they played _____, shared _____ stories and
              board game   *adjective*

examined _____'s tattoo of a _____
          Brady Bunch character   *adjective*

_____.
    noun

Conduct of the Meeting continued (page 120)

After the June 9 meeting concluded, Goldstone apologized to

Trump Jr. According to Goldstone, he told Trump Jr. that he

though there were going to _____ with
verb

_____ and maybe _____ a few
famous singer   *verb*

_____ and told Emin Agalarov in a phone call that
dog breed–plural

the meeting was about adoption and _____
verb ending with ing

_____ _____. He apologized for
color   *child's toy*

_____ his time, and hoped it wouldn't spoil his
verb ending with ing

chances to _____ on the golf course with
verb

_____ next _____. He really liked
Trump family member   *holiday*

_____ at the _____ parade where he could
verb ending with ing   *adjective*

show is _____ pride and dress in _____
noun   *color*

_____ without being judged ... With Veselnitskaya next
dairy product

to him, Kaveladze reported that the meeting had gone well, but

he later told Aras Agalarov that the meeting ... had been a waste

of time ...

Paul Manafort's Campaign-Period Contacts (page 136)

Gates also reported that Manafort instructed him in April 2016 or

early May 2016 to send Kilimnik Campaign internal polling data

and ... share it with the Ukrainian oligarchs. Gates also understood

the information would also be shared with Deripaska, would

share it with _____, who would pass it on to
                    Bond villian

_____, who would give it to _____...
  Disney evil queen   *Spiderman foe*

Gate's account about polling data is consistent with

_____'s plans to _____ the world and
  same Bond villian   *verb*

_____ every single _____
     verb   *adjective*

_____, turning them into _____ cyborgs
  domestic animal   *adjective*

controlled by _____ their brains with _____.
              verb ending with ing   *dessert*

This plan was confirmed with multiple emails that Kilimnik sent to

US associates and press contacts...

Paul Manafort's Meetings (page 140)

Manafort also initially told the Office that he had said to Kilimnik

that the plan was crazy ... Manafort said he didn't want to

_____ any _____ _____ in Russia
    verb   *adjective*   *plural noun*

or _____ He warned too much _____ could
    state in the US .   *pastry item*

cause someone to _____ _____ or even dream
                   verb   *adverb*

about _____ his _____'s
    verb ending with ing   *female relative*

_____. He admitted that he reacted negatively to
   noun

Yanukovych sending – years later – an "urgent" request ...

Manafort ultimately acknowledged Kilimnik also raised the peace

plan in January and February 2017 meetings with Manafort. He

also admitted he liked _____ _____ on
                color   *dairy product*

_____ after _____ his _____
  pastry item   *verb ending with ing*   *adjective*

_____ account.
  social media platform

...Manafort did not refer explicitly to "battleground" states in his

telling of the August 2 discussion. Nor had he mentioned battle-

_____ or warrior _____. He claimed to be
   plural noun   *plural noun*

a _____, not a _____. Though he did admit to
    occupation   *animal*

_____ the occasional _____.
  verb ending with ing   *noun*

Post-Resignation Activities (page 143)

As noted above, _____ gave _____
                 Trump family member   *frozen dessert*

and statements to the Office, Manafort sought to qualify his

engagement on and support for the plan. Originally

_____ wanted to steal a rare _____ from
cartoon character   *noun*

the library of _____, but Manafort suggested they
               city in the US

_____ an infomercial for used _____
    verb   *plural noun*

instead. Kilimnik rejected both plans and while

_____ his _____ with a _____, it
verb ending with ing   *body part*   *noun*

became clear that he really wanted to _____
                                          verb

_____ in their _____. He
2016 Presidential candidate   *room in a house*

wondered if they drove a _____ or rented _____
                          make of car   *color*

_____ to get around. Finally, it was agreed that they
plural noun

would all _____ their favorite _____ and lock
              verb   *noun*

it in a _____and put it under Manafort's
        container

_____.
piece of furniture

Background (page 148)

Nader developed contacts with both U.S. presidential campaigns

during the 2016 election… Dmitriev said that his and the

government of Russia's preference was a candidate Trump to win

and asked Nader to assist him in meeting members of the Trump

Campaign. He wanted to bring them _____ soaked in

plural noun

_____ and wrapped in _____

alcoholic beverage   *foreign country*

_____ from _____ he had seen in

plural noun   *foreign country*

_____. Nader did not introduce Dmitriev to anyone

magazine name

associated with the Trump Campaign before the election.

He was _____ disappointed. He offered to get

adverb

_____ a guest spot on the Russian version of

Trump family member

_____ or _____ and fix it so they

game show   *reality competition show*

won. He also knew an _____ artist who would draw

foreign country

them _____ a _____ _____ from

verb ending with ing   *adjective*   *noun*

_____. But they had to be quick, since

clothing store chain

_____ had expressed interest in _____

British royal   *verb ending with ing*

with Dmitriev's _____ and was willing to

noun

_____ _____ in the Kremlin.

verb   *plural noun*

Kirill Dmitriev's Post-Election Contacts (page 149)

Soon after midnight on election night, Dmitriev messaged

_____'s _____ who was travelling to New

Trump family member   *house pet*

York to attend the 2016 World Chess Championship. They had

wagered that _____ would be beat

Star Wars character

_____ in _____ moves while

Star Trek character   *small number*

_____ with his _____ closed. Dmitry

verb ending with ing   *noun*

Peskov, the Russian Federation's press secretary, who was also

attending... was _____ several _____ at

verb ending with ing   *plural noun*

the tournament. He claimed he had won for best _____

noun

but further investigation revealed he lost _____ matches

large number

in a row to _____ and had painted himself

cartoon character

_____ to resemble a _____ assuming no one could

color   *flower*

_____ him while he was _____ his

verb   *verb ending with ing*

_____ chess pieces.

adjective

At approximately 2:40 am on November 9, 2019, news reports

stated that candidate Clinton had called ... Trump to concede. At

that point, he shouted, "_____ _____

adjective   *adjective*

_____, holy _____ _____, I

plural noun   *verb ending with ing*   *dairy product*

can't believe it!" then wrote Dmitriev, "Putin has won."

Prince and Dmitriev Meet in the Seychelles (page 151)

... Nader informed Prince that the Russians were looking to build a

link with the incoming Trump administration.

_____ mentioned he told Prince that Dmitriev
The Sopranos character

had been pushing Nader to introduce him to someone from the

incoming Administration. He was even willing to meet

_____'s _____ teacher or the guy who was
Trump family member   _school subject_

_____ his _____. Nader suggested ... that
verb ending with ing   _noun_

Prince and Dmitiriev meet to discuss issues of mutual concern.

Maybe they could _____ their _____ or try
                  verb   _plural noun_

_____ some _____ _____ in
verb ending with ing   _adjective_   _vegetable–plural_

the _____ of the White House. Prince told Nader that he
    room in a house

needed to think further about it and to check with Transition

Team officials.

The Seychelles Meetings (page 153)

Dmitriev arrived ... in the Seychelles on January 11, 2017... Prince

arrived that same day... The initial meeting lasted approximately

30-45 minutes.

They were both _____ that _____ was in
emotion   *television show*

its final season, and wondered if _____ could revive
famous actor

it by _____ the current cast or maybe
verb ending with ing

_____ some new _____ on
verb ending with ing   *plural noun*

_____. Prince describe the eight years of the Obama
planet

Administration in negative terms... According to Prince, he told

Dmitriev that Bannon was effective if not conventional and that

Prince provided policy papers to Bannon.

His favorite policy was about _____ the
verb ending with ing

_____ _____ in the fields of _____
adjective   *plural noun*   *state in the US*

during the _____ festivals of _____ at which
adjective   *holiday*

many _____ from every _____ within
plural noun   *fast food restaurant*

_____ would gather to _____ their
city in the US   *verb*

_____ _____.
adjective   *plural noun*

The Seychelles Meetings cont'd (page 154)

They spent most of the day _____ in the pool and
verb ending with ing

_____ _____ sea shelles on the Seychelles
verb ending with ing   *adjective*

beach. Dmitiriev challenged Prince to say that _____ times
large number

_____ while drinking a _____ _____,
adverb   *adjective*   *nationality*

one of the popular local cocktails. Prince responded by

_____ Dmitriev in the _____ so hard that he
verb ending with ing   *body part*

started to _____ his _____ and nearly
verb   *diufferent body part*

lost his _____ _____. The topic of Russian
adjective   *internal organ*

interference in the 2016 election did not come up.

After a few rounds of _____ the _____ on the
verb   *noun*

_____, they found a local _____ restaurant
noun   *ice cream flavor*

and ended up _____ on the _____
verb ending with ing   *plural noun*

before a local celebrity, _____ _____ and his
adjective   *male name*

wife, _____ _____ asked them to leave. Prince
adverb   *female name*

added the would inform Bannon about his meeting with

Dmitriev... He wished Dmitriev a _____ _____,
adjective   *holiday*

changed his _____ and flew off like a _____
noun   *type of bird*

chased by a _____.
wild animal

The Seychelles Meetings cont'd (page 154-155)

At the second meeting, Prince told Dmitriev that the US could not

accept any Russian involvement in Libya because it would make

the situation there much worse. _____ got his
Trump family member

_____ from there and didn't want any _____
noun   *adjective*

_____ from Russian _____ it up. Also, he
noun   *verb ending with ing*

didn't want to miss the latest episode of _____.
                          soap opera

That would make him _____ and he'd have to
           emotion

_____ a _____ under the _____ if
verb   *noun*   *piece of furniture*

that happened.

After the brief second meeting concluded … Dmitriev told Nader

that he was disappointed … he believed the Russians need to be

communicating with someone who had more authority… Second,

he had hoped to have a discussion of greater substance …

Dmitriev told Nader that he could _____ _____
                          adverb   *verb*

Prince's comments, and his _____ jokes and
               nationality

_____ singing were insulting to all forms of
adjective

_____ _____.
adjective   *plural noun*

Carter Page Contact with … Dvorkovich (page 166)

In December 2016, more than two months after he was removed

from the Trump Campaign, former Campaign foreign policy

advisor Carter Page again visited Moscow in an attempt to purse

business opportunities. As a small _____, he had always
                                           noun

wanted to _____ in _____. This was the
               verb   *foreign country*

_____ opportunity for him to _____ some of
      adjective   *verb*

the _____ who had dismissed him as _____
          plural noun   *adjective*

and _____ when he was _____ on the
        adjective   *verb ending with ing*

campaign … Page also gave some individuals the impression he

had maintained his connections to President-Elect Trump.

On December 9, 2016, Page went to dinner with NES employees

Weber and Krickovic. Weber had contacted Dvorkovich … to invite

him to stop by the dinner … Dvorkovich asked Page if he could

facilitate … a discussion of future cooperation. Page ignored him

and order a big plate of _____ and _____
                            type of meat   *type of vegetable*

covered in _____. He ate so fast it caused him to
              dairy product

_____ his _____ all over his companions.
     verb   *noun*

Potential 1030 Violation by _____ (page 179)
Trump family member

Reports that _____ was caught
same Trump family member

_____ someone else's _____ were
verb ending with ing · *noun*

determined to be _____. Nonetheless, it was the
adjective

_____ duty of the Office to _____ any possible
adjective · *verb*

violations of section 1030, which clearly stated it was

_____ to _____ while _____ or
adjective · *verb* · *verb ending with ing*

to _____ a _____ against its will. And such
verb · *noun*

acts were _____ mentioned in context with
adverb

_____.
same Trump family member

Applying the Principles of Federal Prosecution, however, the

Office determined that prosecution of this potential violation was

not warranted … However, _____ is a
same Trump family member

_____ jerk, and just because we can't _____
adjective · *verb*

sufficiently to _____ enough _____ doesn't
verb · *plural noun*

mean there isn't a _____ reason to _____
adjective · *verb*

anyone caught _____ with the Office.
verb ending with ing

Constitutional Considerations (page 190)

Finally, the First amendment could pose constrains on a

prosecution of _____ since the right to

Trump family member

_____ is _____ in our constitution, and our

verb   *adjective*

forefathers fought _____ to _____ that right

      adverb   *verb*

and preserve it for future _____. As much as The

      plural noun

Office wants to _____ the _____ involved in

      verb   *plural noun*

this _____ crime, we have to follow this _____

      adjective   *adjective*

law stuff and can't _____ any _____ that we

      verb   *plural noun*

want. It's not fair. I am a *special* counsel, and should be able to

view any _____ I deem necessary to _____

      noun   *verb*

this very _____ investigation. Anything less is the same

      adjective

as _____ your mother's _____ and then

      verb ending with ing   *noun*

lying about it. Maybe there's a typo in the first amendment and

they really meant the right to _____ _____

      verb   *plural noun*

shall not be abridged. Anyway, my _____ is tied, and I

      body part

cannot, by law, _____ as much as I want to.

      verb

_____.I

expletive

Constitutional Considerations cont'd (page 191)

The Office has found previously undiscovered articles in the

constitution that may be relevant to the investigation. They

specifically say that _____ during a campaign can be
_____ *verb ending with ing*

_____ and considered treasonous. It also gives the
adjective

Special Counsel the power to _____ any
verb

_____ that they deem may be _____. We
noun   *adjective*

interpret this to mean we are as powerful as _____,
comic book superhero

and _____ tall buildings, are more _____ than
verb   *adjective*

a speeding bullet, and can bend _____ with our bare
plural noun

hands. It's right there in the constitution.

The Office also assumes the power to _____ any
verb

television show, to be a _____ force for _____
adjective   *emotion*

in our nation's _____, and make sure every
fast food restaurant—plural

_____ in this country is _____ their
noun   *verb ending with ing*

_____. We are Special, we are Counsel, we are
body part—plural

_____ awesome.
adjective

_____ **(page 194)**
Trump family member

According to witnesses, _____ was
same Trump family member

responsible for _____ most of the _____
verb ending with ing   *plural noun*

at the Clinton Campaign. They also pranked the opposition at

every opportunity, _____ fake orders for
verb ending with ing

_____, gluing their _____ to their
takout food   *plural noun*

_____, and setting up fake _____ dating
plural noun   *adjective*

profiles.

One profile for Hillary described her as a _____ woman
adjective

who liked _____ flowers, _____
verb ending with ing   *verb ending with ing*

_____, and watching _____
fast food menu item   *adjective*

_____ films starring _____. It also
movie genre   *famous actor*

claimed she swam _____ miles every day, liked
large number

_____ in a hammock, and enjoyed cooking
verb ending with ing

_____ _____ in a _____ sauce. In this
adjective   *zoo animal*   *color*

profile, she was looking for a _____ man with no
adjective

_____ who can _____ while
body part   *verb*

_____ in his _____ pajamas.
verb ending with ing   *cartoon character*

No one responded to the fake profile.

Others Interviewed During the Investigation (pages 198-199)

The Office considered whether, during the course of the

investigation, other individuals interviewed either omitted

material information or provided information determined to be

false … the Office did not seek criminal charges against any

individuals other than those listed above …

But, that doesn't mean that they weren't _____
                                           verb ending with ing

about their _____ activities and trying to
            adjective

_____ us. They think they're so _____, but
    verb   *adjective*

we're more _____ and even if we don't find any
          same adjective

incriminating _____ now, that doesn't mean we won't,
            noun

so we'll keep _____ our _____ off until
            verb ending with ing   *body part—plural*

we catch them _____ or they _____ a
            verb ending with ing   *verb*

_____ or _____ to the wrong
    noun   *verb*

_____ or something else against the law. We're
    noun

_____ you, just like _____.
verb ending with ing   *mythical holiday character*

73

Volume II

The Trump Campaign Reacts to WikiLeaks … (page 17-18)

Within the Trump Campaign, aides reacted with enthusiasm to

reports of the hacks. _____ and _____
Marvel superhero   DC superhero

discussed with Campaign officials that WikiLeaks would release

hacked material. Some witnesses said that Trump himself

discussed the possibility of upcoming releases _____
verb ending with ing

Clinton and causing her to _____. Michael Cohen, then
verb

executive vice-president of the Trump Organization … recalled

hearing _____ _____ and dancing
Trump family member   verb ending with ing

when the _____ hacked material was posted on
adjective

WikiLeaks and _____-lovers.com. They also offered
fruit

prayers to their god, _____ and sacrificed several
video game character

_____ on an altar made of _____ and
plural noun   noun

covered in _____. Cohen recalled that Trump
dairy product

responded, "oh good, alright," and "merry _____ you
holiday

_____ animals."
adjective

The Trump Campaign Reacts to WikiLeaks ... cont'd (page 18)

Manafort said that shortly after WikiLeak's July 22 2016 release of

hacked documents, he spoke to Trump about _____
                                          verb ending with ing

the _____ so that they could _____ in
      noun   *verb*

_____ and make even more _____ in the
state in the US   *noun*

_____; Manafort recalled that Trump responded that
room in a house

Manafort should _____ his own _____ and
                    verb   *noun*

keep Trump updated. Deputy campaign manager Rick Gates said

that Manafort was getting pressure about _____ the
                                          verb ending with ing

adjective _____ and _____ information and
            noun   *adjective*

that Manafort instructed Gates to _____ every
                                    verb

_____ he saw when _____ status updates
noun   *verb ending with ing*

on the upcoming releases. Around the same time, Gates was with

Trump on a trip to an airport in _____ where they
                                  foreign country

picked up a case of _____ for _____'s
                      noun   *Trump family member*

birthday and received a call from _____ who
                                   Game of Thrones character

warned him that _____ was _____, and
                  season   *verb ending with ing*

shortly after the call ended, Trump told Gates that more releases

of damaging information would be coming.

Conduct Towards Flynn, Manafort, _____ (page 120)
Seinfeld character

In addition to the interactions with McGahn described above, the

president has taken other actions directed at possible witnesses in

the special Counsel's investigation, including Flynn, Manafort,

_____ – who would just show up and
same Seinfeld character

_____ from time to time just to make the President
verb

_____ – and … Cohen. During Manafort's prosecution …
verb

the President repeatedly stated that Manafort was being treated

unfairly and … could receive a pardon. He also promised to give

him _____ _____ if he could keep from
large number   *plural noun*

_____ the _____ _____ and that
verb ending with ing   *adjective*   *noun*

jail wasn't so bad in the _____ parts of _____
adjective   *state in the US*

because they gave you free _____ and you could dress
plural noun

up as your favorite _____ character and
Saturday morning cartoon show

make your own _____ cheese.
adjective

_____ the _____ page (128)
verb ending with ing   *noun*

In addition to pardons, Trump would offer _____
adjective

_____ to anyone who would _____ his
plural noun   *verb*

_____. He also promised to _____ every last
body part   *verb*

_____ on the _____ if they would bring
noun   *NFL team name*

him _____ on his birthday. He said he could make
plural noun

them _____, and even get them on TV on shows like,
adjective

"Meet the _____" and " _____ for
plural noun   *verb ending with ing*

Dollars." Alternatively, he would threaten to _____
verb

anyone who didn't say "the Apprentice" was the _____
adjective

show ever. Sometimes, late at night, when the

_____ roamed the halls of _____, he
wild animal–plural   *famous building*

would tell stories of _____ _____ when
verb ending with ing   *plural noun*

he was a boy. He would also _____ his _____
verb   *noun*

until the sun rose, then watch reruns of _____ and
television show

brag about the size of his _____.
noun

81

The President Sends Messages of Support to Cohen (page 146)

A few days after the searches ... the President encouraged Cohen

to "hang in there" and "stay strong." Cohen also recalled that ...

he heard from individuals who ... relayed the President's support

for him. Cohen recalled that _____, a friend of the
Marvel Avenger

President, reached out to say that he was with "the Boss" in Mar-

a-Lago and the President said "he loves you" and not to worry.

Cohen recalled that the _____prime _____
adjective *adjective*

_____ of the secret section known as the
military rank

_____ _____ for the Trump Organization,
adjective *plural noun*

told him, "the boss loves you." And Cohen said that a man

dressed as a _____ who spoke with a _____
zoo animal *adjective*

accent and gave sweet _____ to the children, a friend
plural noun

of the President's, told him, "everyone knows the boss has your

back."

Made in the USA
San Bernardino, CA
12 May 2019